# Conversations From My Head

*By*
*Alero Irene Familusi*

# Table of Contents

# Dedication

To my grandparents, who encouraged me to be all I could be and showed me what was possible. And Grandpa – my Best Man, your stories and rich expressions were my first impression of poetry.

Sun re o!

# Acknowledgment

In the words of Uncle Snoop, first, I'd like to thank me, for getting off the couch of procrastination and finally getting this done.

But honestly, I'm grateful to all those who lent both overt and covert support. Starting with an eternal and unconditional companion who, despite my inconsistency, God has been more faithful than I deserve.

Husband man – Folarin: Sturdy anchor, I know this is not your forte, but for everything else and supporting my currently jobless self, thank you. For your humour and eternal optimism in the absence of any evidence to support it, and I love you.

Iya Alero – you have been both wúrà and dígí. My life story is incomplete without you! You've shown me what strength looks like; I'm still taking lessons in letting go and forgiveness.

Pamilerinayo and Opemipo – The absolute loves and joys of my life. You both taught me lessons in patience but also showed me how boundless love can be. You both make me want to be everything and more, so you can be the impossible! I hope you can both read this someday and not find it cringe.

Mosh & Tesh – Friends bestowed on me from above by blood. Omo ìyá mi, my cheerleaders. You both make me feel like I can do anything, no matter how stupid it might sound.

Adedoyin mi òwón, my sister from another mother, your encouragement and friendship have defied oceans and borders.

Susu – unbelievably supportive and eternal sunshine. I'm grateful you called my name that day in the chemist, and you haven't stopped calling me or calling me out since, even when you're not at your best, you don't stop giving of yourself.

Brutally honest Akin, old friends are the best friends. Thank you for your support. We shall drink the ogogoro when the book is out.

And to the Amazon team – Daisy, Cheryl, Alex, John, Zayn and everyone else who was on this project, thank you. It only took almost 2 years, but your persistence won over my self-doubt and procrastination.

And finally, to everyone who ever shared their feelings or thoughts with me, or let me share mine, to all those who shared my space, even for a moment and those who chose to remain here. I don't have that many people in my life, but my people are "MY PEOPLE", and even if I left out your name on this page, you are in my heart, and I am grateful!

# About the Author

Alero Familusi was born in Ilorin and schooled and lived there with her grandparents till she finished secondary school. The second of three girls, she finished from the University of Ibadan, where she was encouraged by a friend to record her writing. Her first influence in writing was her grandfather and has no writing related education.

She considers herself a reader who loves a good play on words and so dares to write on occasion. Her first "public" attempt at writing was a blog titled random musings of the unhinged mind www.randommusingsoutloud.wordpress.com, a collection of thoughts and some poetry, but this will be her first published book.

Alero lives in England with her husband and 2 gremlins and no other pets.

# Best man

I have often wondered about the concept of the 'best man' by a groom's side at weddings. I was made to understand he had to be someone dependable. Someone both bride and groom could count on and lean on, someone who was certain to come through for them both, no matter what.

This counts as one of the hardest things I've had to do. Write a tribute to my best man…

My grandfather, father, friend, confidant, dependable shoulder, a non-judgmental ear and best man. The best man any girl could wish for. You made all his girls feel special, you raised our standards, so we knew to demand more from life and ourselves. You chastised lovingly with a voice I grew to love, a voice I've never not known until now. A voice I have not heard in 10 years.

You were a most beautiful man, faithful, respectful, dedicated, loyal, and all-round beautiful. Seeing you with granny, showed me how I wanted to be treated. Listening to your stories, they told me who I wanted to be and who I couldn't afford to be. You loved all your girls, unconditionally and completely. That was the man I knew and loved. You weren't infallible, but as accepting of your own few imperfections, as you were of others'.

How then do I write a tribute to such greatness? I don't, can't. I can only say – I lost my best man, and his passing leaves a void, I can only attempt to fill with vivid and pleasurable memories of this most amazing man.

All the world's a stage, and all the men and women merely players.

They have their exits and their entrances, and one man in his time plays many parts…

Grandpa, you exited stage left, and your performance left me in awe and caused me to give a standing ovation. Out, out brief candle, the ones we love are never old enough. Goodnight, sir, till the sun rises again and never sets.

# Eyes Tight Shut

You've been gone too long
But not so long that I forget
I remember it all
All my senses remember them well

Your lips upon mine
Your skin against mine
Your kisses on my back
Your essence inside me

How you kiss me
Like you own me
Like you want me
Like you need me

With eyes tight shut
I can smell you
Taste you, feel you
Eyes tight shut

And then reality jolts me
Eyes wide open
I am reminded
You are not mine to love – Not anymore

# Victory

The nature of violation has evolved
Once recognizable and predictable
Now, it lurks menacingly in the dark
Deceptive in its new form, transformed in the dark of night

Once upon a time, it lurked in shadows
Dressed in a stranger's threatening garb
Now, it knocks on the door as the comforting presence of a familiar face,
Or a kindred spirit with shared intellectual grace

I secured my borders against strangers, kept the aliens at bay
But in welcoming the familiar, I invited in a vampire to ravage and pillage
No longer content with flesh and blood, it lays waste to my soul, my life and my will
And in its wake, it leaves me as nothing, desolate, stealing life's very essence

In my surrender, it claims a second victory
Yet within this surrender, its triumph is for a moment
Then I remember, his second victory is mine to give
But today, I'm weary, so I concede
Tomorrow? Tomorrow, the cycle is renewed – we war again

# November

November of the orange leaves and harmattan dust
November of the early morning fogs, a forerunner to Christmas
November, once my favourite time of year, the time I celebrated me
I was enough reason to make it the best month of the year

Then it happened, she happened.
Thanatos visited and November was never the same again.
In place, the beauty of the fire-coloured leaves, I see brown and rot
on dark pavement.
Instead of being in awe of the mysteries that lurk in the fog
I freeze in fear of what evil it may harbour.

The tenacity with which I loved you
Is the degree with which I now loathe it.
November stole from me what would have been my first
What was most pure and precious.
November stole the innocence I bore and didn't let me touch her

In November's embrace, the shadow of the Eternal Embrace cast over
the month,
A gentle reminder of life's fleeting dance.
November, no longer a celebration of joy and cheer,
But a gentle surrender to the tranquil cloak of eternal silence.

# Strong Black Coffee

The melanin-proficient Amun, in his many roles
Dripping with confidence
A god carrying the DNA of his ancestors
You also carry their burdens

Father, brother, lover and friend
Resplendent in passion and strength
He embodies strength and divine authority
And yet your back remains ramrod straight

Protector, pride of the continent
How is it your back is bent and strained
Your will weakened
Who has broken you?

# Tonight

Tonight, I commit pen to paper
For one is the dancer, and the latter the stage
Not just for use of ink
But to transform thoughts into substance

Tonight,
Not a myriad of thoughts
Not a billion stars
Not a thousand laughs
Not innumerable sand
Not a legion of demons

Tonight,
What I feel I choose not to fight
One thought in this heart
One moon in this vast sky
One reason in this world

Tonight,
These thoughts come to life.
From my mind through my hands on to pulp

# Body Beautiful

Beautiful is not how I'd describe my body
It's a map, a detailed journal of my journey
A journey that wasn't always smooth.
Every scar, visible or hidden, tells a tale.
The tales are woven into a story
The story woven is makes me, me
My body isn't beautiful, says my mind.
My mind, as convoluted as train tracks, isn't ashamed of this body.
It is unapologetic, objective of what it is.
I am at peace with my scars; we're well acquainted.
My mind knows, "she is, because they are."
This version of me does not exist without my old friends.
My mind looks at my body and chronicles each scar,
It reminisces over every battle and counts my losses as lessons.
My mind looks upon my scars with pride.
It reminds me the journey isn't over – "remain battle-ready," she
says.
There's still space for more scars, and they'll be just as beautiful
My body isn't beautiful, her scars are.

# Colourless

Today, the world is neither black nor white
Woke up to a world of different shades of grey
Today, the sun found Gaia unworthy of her golden presence,
It remains hidden behind the clouds, shrouded by a curtain of tears
The tears fall torrentially from the skies; nature mirrors my emotions.

Today, I see no smiles
Every face is drawn,
Every eye filled with tears
Because the rainbow is gone, leaving a world devoid of colour.

Today, I am reminded that death is real
Interment hits me with the finality and reality of death
Today, a child is born
Today, a mother buried
The irony does not escape me
They call it the cycle of life
Smiles and tears on different faces in one day
But today, I see no colours, only grey.

# Tunnels

When one door closes, somewhere, a window opens
I look through, and it's the same empty blackness
Daring me to come through, to explore its frightening uncertainty
I've been walking for years; it seems someone forgot to turn on
the lights at the end of the tunnel, 'cos it's still as dark as the day I
started

Yes, like I'm right back where I started
I'm still falling
Further and faster into the dark abyss
There's no net beneath me
Still sinking, sir!!!

In this tumultuous ocean
The raging seas
There's no straw to clutch at
No branch or twig to hang on to
It broke off when despair showed up
Hope failed to grow anew, a branch

Fall, drown, walk
I go, not knowing where
I cry, not knowing why
I speak, not knowing what
I trust, knowing not in who

# Blind Justice

Freedom has never been less free
Truly, none is more bound
Justice is neither just nor fair
Only selectively blind
Freedom is subdued, but tyranny reigns supreme
Liberty untethered in the grasp of the untrained
Truly chaos is at home; come once more to mock the pretence of
freedom
To jeer at Justice's blindness
While we sit silently and mourn the demise of order

# Unyielding Abyss

It's back again!!!! The dark, faceless ogre
It's back to torment me
To drag me down to the pit of despair
Upon its return, it has garnered more strength
With jagged claws, it tugs at the corners of my heart
With sharp teeth, it gnaws painfully at my soul
Within me, a consuming force, it moves
In its wholeness, it moves within me
Consuming, absorbing, relentless, unyielding
Despair has gained permanence, an eternal desolation, an unvanquished shadow.

# Another Time

I come from a simpler time, a different time
A time when black was black and white was white
And both were mere colours, open to the greys and pinks
Black and white, where just keys on a piano

I come from a different time, a simpler time
When boys were boys and girls were girls
We were different only because boys stood while we had to sit
And we dreamt of dolls, while they played with guns

Now, my dreams are different
Dreams for a colour-blind world
A gender indifferent people
Where colours remained just that, and gender didn't define one

I wish for a simpler time
When black and white were colours
Gender was a part of speech
And I... a product of my works alone.

# See You Never...

I want a quick visit to a place not here

To see people, I'll never meet again and the one who never got to meet me.

How could you know someone you never saw?

Yet shared so much with, every life's cord

We both savoured the same delicacies

But you chose what we abhorred

What could 1 have done to make you stay?

What did I do to make you leave?

How does my heart still bleed?

How is the dam of my soul broken so it streams down my face?

I wish I held your tiny hands once, I wish I got to kiss your sweet face

But I can't, I didn't

It will have to do till a time when there is no end.

# My Friend, The Lizard

It's been a while, my friend
I see your smiles on Instagram, your accomplishments on LinkedIn
I read your thoughts on Twitter and laugh at your dance moves on
Tiktok
Your memes and forwarded messages on WhatsApp make me laugh
or introspect
It's been a while, my friend
Clearly too long, because I read your obituary today and realise I can't
remember your voice
It occurs to me that we haven't had honest conversation in a while
I haven't called to know how you're really doing
I saw the beautiful pictures on social media and assumed you were
well
You who cracked our ribs, hid the cracks beneath the surface
We who you made laugh, couldn't tell how you were hurting
My friend was the lizard lying flat on his stomach; I couldn't tell he
had a bellyache

# Old Love

Old love, new love
No matter, forbidden love
As I lay me down to sleep
I open my eyes, and it's you next to me
Then I shut them close
Cos it can't be true
Only a projection of my illusions
Only delusions of my thoughts
Old love, new love
No matter – forbidden love

# Bye Lover

Hey lover, how are you doing today, lover?
I missed you last night while you were asleep. No, this is not to say
how much I love you, because you already know.
You know how you sow seeds in my head and reap in my loins.
You know how you're my every waking thought
You know how you seep into my thoughts, taking over my mind.
No, this isn't to tell you what you already know.
Hey lover, how are you doing today, lover? I miss you even now, as
I write and you aren't here.
Yes, this is to tell you the things you don't know
That you are a beautiful distraction, I can scarcely afford
That you take over my thought process, and I barely function
I'm leaving because I love you so much; I've lost me

# Perfect Match

You and I are alike
The Ying to my Yang
The Clyde to my Bonnie
Stormy one minute and sunny the next
Grey and dull for a moment, and bright and cherry right after

# Smells Like Home

As I get off the plane and walked towards the arrival hall, I am welcomed most unpleasantly by the ever-so-familiar stench of slowly fermenting urine.

I am reminded, almost instantly, of the things I do not miss about home and almost begin to long for the less familiar scents of blossom trees from a place that is not home.

Then, I am rudely reminded by my heart that those scents mark a different kind of smell.

The putrid miasma of aloneness

The effluvium of exclusion

The reek of non-communal living

Odours that hurt not my nose but my heart,

Smells that cause self-doubt and cause me to question all I thought I knew of myself

Scents that are confined not to select locations but diffuse all through the monarchy

I remember the unpleasant fragrance of cold winters and even colder mortals, then I submit to the welcoming scent of slowly fermenting urine with its promise of warmth and inclusion – with a promise of communal, over-concerned busybodies.

## No One's Home

Knock Knock
Who's there?
Clearly not me – I haven't been home in a while
Can you see me?
Can you hear me? Or am I just air
Maybe then you can feel me
Tell me, do you still care?

# Where Is She?

Who is she who is here now?

Talented, amazing, shining, different…

Uncomfortable?

Who was she before now?

Talented, amazing, shining, different…

Comfortable?

Who you were before now was just as amazing; the world just didn't see it

Don't be carried away by the applause

People are too fickle, and this is just another moment

You who knows you should celebrate you

Don't wait for us to catch up

Go ahead and celebrate all of who you are, all of who you were

Who you've become was always there, brewing under the surface of who you were

Do not despise who you were; she was a foundation for who you've become

Applaud her, celebrate her

Where is she who was here before?

Bubbling under the surface

# Disrobe

Take it off!!! All of it!
It's hideous
Doesn't suit you
It's a lie

Take all of it off!!!
You look better without it
You'll feel better without it
I promise

Take it all off
Then breathe
That mask, the pretence, the lie
Discard them, let them burn

Take it all off, then feel it all
That's the truth
It's lighter
It won't kill you

This mask, the facade
It serves no one
Not anymore.
Take off the girdle of correctness and breathe.

# Oní Dìrí

I sit in the backseat of yeye's yellow Toyota Corolla
My heart pounding so loud, I hear it in my head
My brain thumping with dread
The blood coursing through my veins at the speed of light

No, I'm not in trouble
It's the time of the week
The hairstyle for next week is kò l'ésè
I've drawn the short straw; ìyàwó will not be making my hair this
week

Iya Taofeek is no mean woman
Her hands make my plaits just as tight and migraine-inducing as i
ìyàwó
So, no, I am not afraid of her
It is not her hands I fear

She is ready for me now
I assume position on a tiny wooden stool with four stumpy legs
She sits on a higher chair with Iro and Buba facing me
She starts by combing my hair with that wooden comb
And then, with no fear of God, grabs my head firmly between her
thighs

Then the tears are silently falling down my face
It is not the pain from the combing
Nor from the sharp ìlarun making straight, precise lines on my head
No, it is the smell from her nether regions
The smell like brined fish is what assails my nostrils

I bear the smell and pain for another 67 minutes
Yes, I counted each minute
She's done and hands me a small broken piece of the mirror to admire
her intricate work on my head.
It is indeed beautiful, but is it worth it?
My solace? Next week – we swap
My sister endures the stench, and all I must deal with is the pain

# Enduring Gloom

You're always there, lurking in the dark
Residing in the shadows
Tethered precariously on the precipice
Threatening to break the dam
Ominously teetering on the brink of ruin

How are you so strong? Ever present?
Why are you not chased away by the light?
How is your darkness so overbearing?
Your weight so ponderous, knocking me out of orbit

Hello sadness, my old friend
It seems I cannot separate you from me, or me from you
Can you in your mercy evoke compromise
Let this light through, but for a minute so I can smile

# Buttercup Cloud

I'm not black or white,
People are not a monochrome of pigments,
People are a homogenous mixture of dyes,
A myriad of different shades, even in the same hue.

I fill a form, and I'm asked if I'm black,
I ask, "black?" Black like coffee or a panther?
I can't relate, I don't see it,
I can't say I've met many who are "black."

My confusion leads me to Dulux,
I think to colour-match,
"Dulux, Dulux on the web, what colour would you say I am?"
Clear is thy hue, and Buttercup Cloud is what I see.

I ask again in the summer,
When the fiery ball has roasted me a tad more golden,
"Dulux, Dulux on the web, what colour would you say I am?"
Again, it tells me, "Clear is thy hue, but alas! Now you are Pharaoh's
Gold 5."

I am not a monochrome of black or white,
Dulux says I am much more,
I am not one or the other stripe of a zebra,
I am magnificent Pharaoh's Gold and sometimes sublime Buttercup
Cloud.

I go back to the form,
Hoping to find either glorious option,
But alas, I'm stuck with Black.

# Death By Marriage

"I do."
And so it was, with those two little words and an unfortunate big smile, she pronounced her own sentence.
The penalty – death by marriage.

Dreams, hopes and aspirations sacrificed on the altar of marriage,
Murdered by mini-hers and hims that drilled through her to become.
Untimely ended by routine,
Vanquished by daily expectations and societal demands

"I don't,"
The magic words that resurrected her soul.
"I don't give up, I don't retreat, I don't shrink,"
Her voice finally comes through, and she hears her own self.

Finally, her voice isn't just a whisper,
Her strength is renewed,
Her not-so-little bundles of joy have reminded her,
She is awakened to her purpose – she remembers who she was meant to be.

# Yesterday

Yesterday ended last night,
But its nightmares creep into my today,
Haunting and crippling its reality.

Tomorrow doesn't begin till then,
But it's anxieties,
They disable my present.

Today,
There's no time left for it,
For it has all been spent,
Worrying about the past and future.

# Goodnight

How has it been so long?
To die is never to have lived
To die is to leave behind no traces of you,
How is it possible…

For one who lived so much to die?
For one who loved so much to be extinguished?
For one who gave so much bow out so silently?
Our existence is indeed nothing but vanity.

"See you tomorrow" is, at best, presumptive optimism.
Setting your alarm is a gamble,
"We'll talk about it later" is an arrogant prediction of an unlived
future,
Remember, tomorrow is promised to no one.
Live easy, till we all answer nature's call.

# Once Upon A Time

Ah!!! Sweet memories,
I had them once,
Before I was touched by life,
Life has laid its cruel hands on what was pure joy.

The river that once nourished,
Now, floods and drowns,
The winds that refreshed?
Replaced with tsunamis and hurricanes.

The sun that replenished?
Now, only scorches and burns.
The earth that once bore newness,
Now, its only joy is to bury.

# Longer Than Forever

As long as God remains sovereign,
As long as the earth has been,
As long as it takes the oceans to dry,
Longer than the Israelite journey,
I'll remain true.

As long as His word remains,
As much as the sands on the shore,
As much as the stars above,
As infinite as a black hole,
I will love you.

More constant than the sun in the sky,
Surer than the earth's rotation,
More than a girl's love for fun,
More than my country's debt,
Is my love.

Longer than Methuselah lived,
Longer than it took the flood to clear,
Larger than Mans struggle.
Will my love remain.

# Perfect Match

You and I are alike,
The Ying to My Yang,
The Clyde to my Bonnie,
Stormy one minute and sunny the next.

Grey and dull for a moment, and bright and cherry right after,
A harmonious cacophony of sounds,
A beautiful contradiction,
A perfect match.

# Vows

Come with me,
Whither... Even I have no knowledge,
Take my hand, and I will lead you.
Have no bother that I can't see my way.

Come away with me,
Bother not, that I have no shelter to lay one head, much less two,
Love me,
Though I may lack a farthing.

Let me plan for us,
Though beyond my nose, I cannot see,
Trust me to care for you,
Though I may be weak of meat and spirit.

Consider me balm,
Though in pain,
It writhe.

For on that Saturday morn,
That is what we swore before God and men,
When we each said "I do."

# Me Against The Elements

I can't stand the rain against my lids,
Nor the pounding of the thunder in my heart,
I can't fight the storm,
That rages within my soul.

All the elements gather against me.
How do I fight that which should sustain me?
How futile the effort?
How hopeless the thought.

The sun once shone on me.
Now, it scorches,
The rain fell silently against my window,
Now, it beats heavily against me.

I am drenched, beat and scorched,
Yet these arms once gave shelter,
Now, they crush and smother,
Now, they cause me grief.

# Let's Pretend

Fly like the sky was boundless,
Sing like no one else could hear,
Roam as though there were no beasts in the jungle,
Walk like the sands on life's shore went on forever.
Laze, as though the sun could never scorch,
Bathe, like He heavens never damned,
Give, like your source was inexhaustible.
Run as though you'd never run out of breath,
Hope, like all your dreams, could only come to pass,
Love, like hearts, could never break,
Live like there only was today.

# Between The Lines

I held out an olive branch,
You insisted I hold up a white flag,
I showed up with a smile,
Your scorching face frowned back at me,
Mine arms I stretched out in comrade,
Your thunderous fury, you unleashed on me.
So, I cry out in pain,
I resign with abandon,
Frustrated at your rejection,
I ask questions,
Expecting no replies,
Then you whisper to my soul,
"Those showers were blessings."
"I sent the sun to dry your tears."
"I asked that you surrender to me because I'm already at peace with
you."

# Wolves At The Door

Lonesome on a hill,
This house, a yawning vacuum,
Loneliness looms large, more real than ever,
Silence wraps me in a forced embrace.

Sunrays scatter, painting the wall in gold,
A gentle breeze glides through open panes,
The dust pirouettes, caught in a prism of light,
An enchanting ballet of hues-fragile and fleeting.

Yet...
Outside this threshold,
The madness of this shadowed globe lurks,
It's cold, cruel hands, eager to claim,
All news is bad news, spilled like ink across polished floors,
Blaring from the wooden box,
Swarming beneath the threshold.

Where do I turn when the wolves encircle?
To whom do I run when my rivers dry and the heavens won't answer?
What do I do,
When the wolves are at my door?

# Like My Favourite Song

Recurring in my mind,
Ever present in my thoughts,
Resounding on my lips,
Like my favourite song,
Wake up with you on my mind,
My last thought at night,
Playing over and over again.

Your name on my lips,
Your face in my dreams,
Your hands on my heart,
Your kisses on my soul,
Like my favourite song,
Memories of you tune the rhythm of senses,
Composing my heart's favourite song.

# Silent Echoes

Like the warmth or a kind sun kissing the nape of her neck,
Not the harsh harmattan glare, scorching and scalding,
Like dew drops at dawn to glisten on the rose's velvet petals,
Not the baleful storm, leaving death and ruin in its wake,
Like a gentle breeze, soothing and cooling, are my memories of an
innocence lost – fragile, fleeting.
A tapestry woven from whispers of days long gone,
Before, shadows stretched long, and storms encroached and camped,
Memories, sweet and haunting, loiter, like echoes of a tune that deigns
to fade,
Carried on the wind, eternal, unshattered.

# Old Foe

Loneliness is my taskmaster,
Misery – its whip,
Depression, the ball and chain,
Keeping me under
Drowning me in a sea, a sadness.
I had forgotten the feeling; the terrain had become strange
Now it creeps back, with its long hands reaching from the shadows,
It grips my heart, and it leaks from my face,
My eyes bleed, and my sail aches.

# Open Secrets

The winds whisper to the trees,
The waves caress the sand,
The soil, intimate with roots of the Jasmin,
Nature has mastered the art of keeping its secrets.

But mine is out in the open,
My heart on my face,
My secrets are out,
I love you.

# Of Love And Angels

Perhaps I never suckled at your bosom,
Yet, from its milk of love and kindness, I was fed.
Perhaps your womb did not birth me,
Yet you sheltered me with core and tenderness.
Your heart – it gave selflessly of you to me,
Teaching me the meaning of love.
Grandmother, yes – the grandest and greatest,
You did so much,
Birthed such love,
That, for you, death is only a transition,
Perhaps now, you may teach even angels to love,
6 feet, 6 aeons cannot erode,
The memories of you I hold dear.